Popocatépetl
and Iztaccíhuatl
A Myth from Mexico

Retold by Joey Acra

NATIONAL GEOGRAPHIC LEARNING

CENGAGE Learning

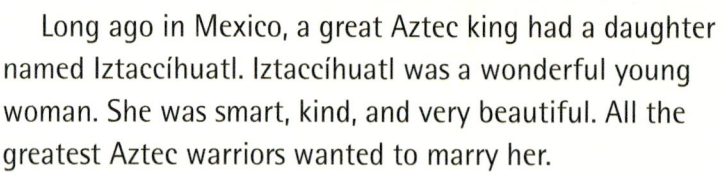

Long ago in Mexico, a great Aztec king had a daughter named Iztaccíhuatl. Iztaccíhuatl was a wonderful young woman. She was smart, kind, and very beautiful. All the greatest Aztec warriors wanted to marry her.

But Iztaccíhuatl loved only one warrior. His name was Popocatépetl.

Popocatépetl was the greatest of all the Aztec warriors and the leader of the king's army.

Popocatépetl loved Iztaccíhuatl, too.

At that time, enemy warriors were attacking the Aztecs. They were destroying villages and killing many of the people because they wanted the Aztecs' land.

The king called Popocatépetl to his palace.

"Our people need you," the king said. "You and your army must go and fight this enemy. If you defeat our enemy, I will allow you to marry my daughter."

Popocatépetl was very happy.

But Iztaccíhuatl didn't want Popocatépetl to go.

"If you go, I'm afraid you will be killed!" she said. "I am afraid I will lose you forever!"

Popocatépetl tried to reassure her.

"No one will kill me," he said. "I will return. Then I will marry you, and we will be together forever!"

Popocatépetl kissed Iztaccíhuatl and said goodbye. Then he left to fight the enemy.

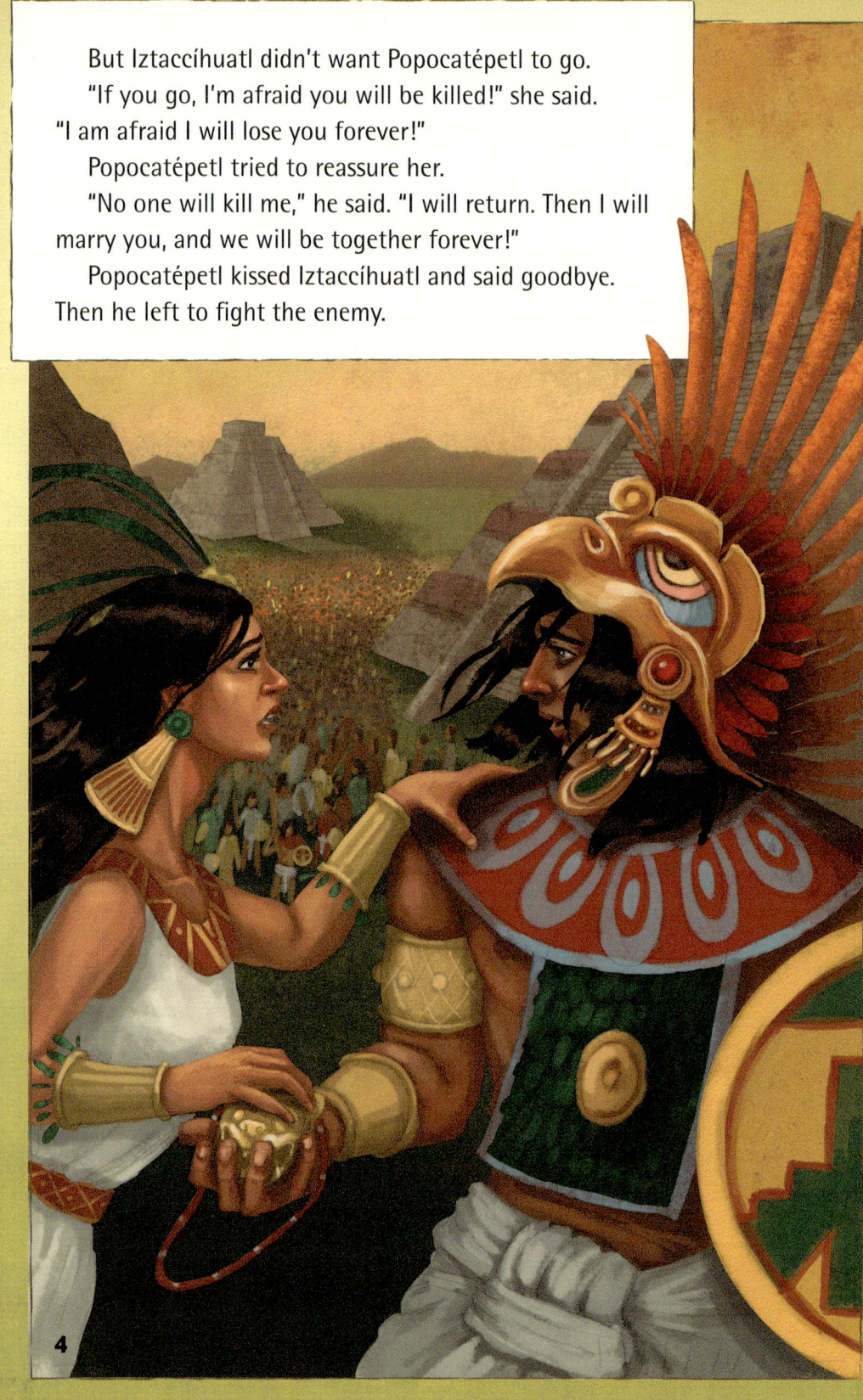

"If I lose him, I'll die from grief," Iztaccíhuatl cried.

Weeks passed, and Iztaccíhuatl waited and worried.

Finally, a messenger arrived.

"Popocatépetl's army defeated the enemy," said the messenger. "He fought bravely, and his army killed many enemy warriors. But I also have terrible news. As he was fighting, an enemy arrow shot Popocatépetl in the heart. He died as he fought to protect his people."

Iztaccíhuatl fell into her father's arms and started to cry.

Iztaccíhuatl was filled with grief. She cried day after day for her lost love. She did not eat. She did not drink. She grew thin and pale.

The king did not know what to do.

"My daughter is dying because I sent Popocatépetl to fight," he said. "But I had no other choice. I had to protect my people."

After days of not eating or drinking, Iztaccíhuatl became sick with a terrible fever. None of the king's doctors could help her.

Three days later, she closed her eyes and died.

But just as Iztaccíhuatl died, loud shouts of excitement came from outside the palace.

"He's back!" a palace guard shouted. "Popocatépetl is back!"

It *was* Popocatépetl! He was not dead!

And now he was back and looking for his love, Iztaccíhuatl.

Popocatépetl raced up the palace steps to see his love. He ran through the palace to Iztaccíhuatl's room.

But when he got to the door, he saw her lifeless body.

"I am sorry," said the king. "She thought that you were dead. She was so sad. She died of grief."

The great warrior looked at Iztaccíhuatl's lifeless body and exploded with anger and grief.

"NO!" he cried. "Why did I leave her?"

NO!

Popocatépetl carried Iztaccíhuatl to a far off valley surrounded by mountains. It was a sacred place where the Aztec people took their dead.

All day he yelled up to the sky.

"Iztaccíhuatl! Why did you leave me?" he cried.

Popocatépetl made two mounds of earth. He placed Iztaccíhuatl on one mound. He laid down on the other.

Popocatépetl ate nothing.

He drank nothing.

Three days later, he died, too.

The Aztec gods looked down from the sky.

"Popocatépetl was a great warrior," they said. "We must honor him and his great love. We will turn Popocatépetl and Iztaccíhuatl into two great mountains that roar. Whenever these mountains roar, people will remember them."

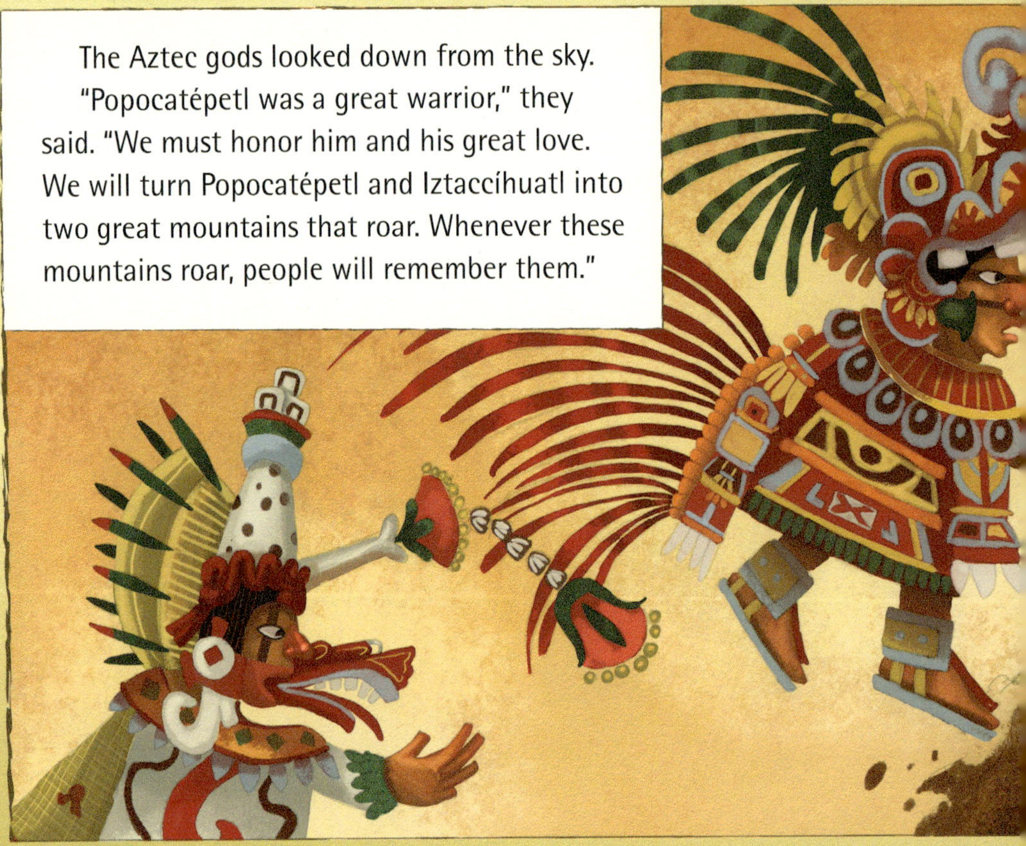

Popocatépetl and Iztaccíhuatl are now together forever, just as Popocatépetl promised Iztaccíhuatl.

The volcano called Iztaccíhuatl is now dormant and sleeps quietly next to the volcano called Popocatépetl.

Popocatépetl sometimes lets out blasts of ash and steam from his crater. The eruptions shake the earth and frighten the people who live nearby.

The gods took the mounds and created two big volcanoes. These were the first volcanoes in Mexico.

The Aztecs called one volcano Iztaccíhuatl, and they called the other Popocatépetl.

When this happens, the people say that Popocatépetl is still yelling at the sky. And he is calling to his great, lost love, Iztaccíhuatl.

Facts About Volcanoes

A volcano is an opening in the Earth's crust through which gas, ash, and hot, melted rock explode. A volcano starts to develop deep beneath the Earth's surface where it is very hot. The heat melts the rock inside the earth. This rock, or magma, rises and blasts out of the ground where it is then called lava. The lava and ash form a mountain around the opening.

A Powerful Force

Volcanoes are one of Earth's most powerful forces. They can shoot lava over 15 meters (about 50 feet) into the air. Lava can reach 1,250 degrees Celsius (2,000 degrees Fahrenheit) and can burn everything in its path, destroying forests and burying cities. But volcanoes can also create new land, and their ash helps keep soil healthy.

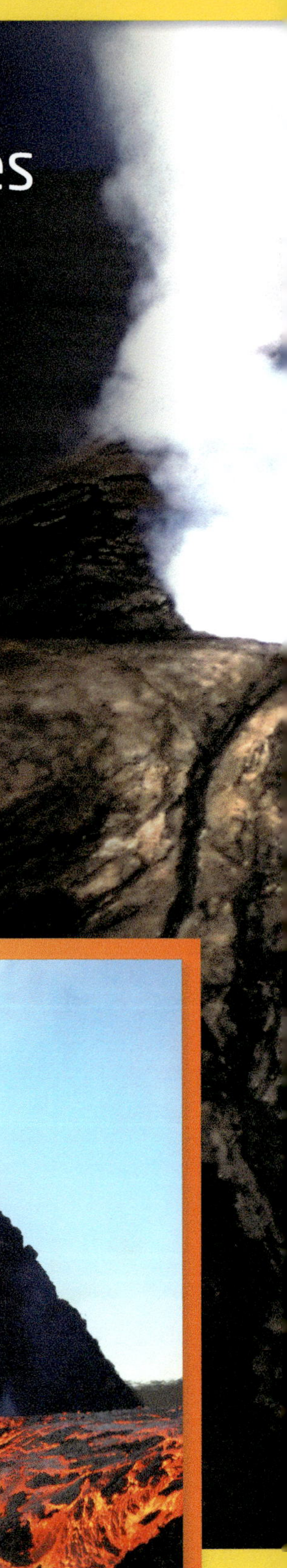

Famous Volcanoes

Today about 1,500 volcanoes on Earth are considered active. Each year about 70 eruptions occur around the world.

Mauna Loa in Hawaii is the world's largest active volcano. More than 97 kilometers (60 miles) wide, it has erupted many times over the past 170 years and could begin to roar again any minute.

Kilauea, also in Hawaii, may be the world's most active volcano. It has been erupting nonstop since January 3,1983.

Krakatau in Indonesia had one of the biggest and loudest eruptions in history in 1883. It has been quiet for years, but no one knows if it will explode again.

Word Play Volcanoes

Use the correct form of the words below to complete the paragraphs. Words can be used more than once.

ash   eruption   dormant   lava   kill

One of the most famous volcanic ___eruptions___ in history happened on the Indonesian island of Krakatau in 1883. After about 200 years of being _____, the Krakatau volcano exploded. The _____ was 13,000 times more powerful than an atomic bomb. The sound was heard over 4,800 kilometers (3,000 miles) away. The eruption _____ more than 36,000 people. _____ from the eruption was carried by wind to places as far away as New York City.

Krakatau collapsed on itself and sank into the ocean. However, in 1927 a new volcano appeared from under the ocean. This volcano sometimes spits hot _____ into the sky. This volcano is called Anak Krakatau, or Child of Krakatau.

Write the word for each picture. Then, on a separate piece of paper, write sentences using each word.

melted   lava   crater   steam

crater

Glossary

army a group of people who fight to protect their country

arrow a stick with a sharp point that is shot from a bow

enemy a group of people that wants to hurt another group of people

grief great sadness

guard a person who protects other people

honor to show that someone is remembered and respected

mounds large piles of earth

palace a large building where people such as kings and queens live

pale colorless and unhealthy looking

promised said that something will happen or that something will be done

reassure to make someone believe that something will be alright

sacred very special and holy

surrounded having something all around

warriors fighters or soldiers